LEUKEMIA

LEUKEMIA

Lorrie Klosterman

 **Marshall Cavendish**
Benchmark
New York

With sincere thanks to Kayla and her family

Marshall Cavendish Benchmark
99 White Plains Road
Tarrytown, New York 10591-9001
www.marshallcavendish.us

This book is not intended for use as a substitute for advice, consultation, or treatment by a licensed medical practitioner. The reader is advised that no action of a medical nature should be taken without consultation with a licensed medical practitioner, including action that may seem to be indicated by the contents of this work, since individual circumstances vary and medical standards, knowledge, and practices change with time. The publisher, author, and medical consultants disclaim all liability and cannot be held responsible for any problems that may arise from use of this book.

Library of Congress Cataloging-in-Publication Data

Klosterman, Lorrie.
  Leukemia / by Lorrie Klosterman.
     p. cm. — (Health alert)
  Includes index.
  Summary: "Discusses leukemia and its effects on people and
society"—Provided by publisher.
  ISBN 0-7614-1916-0
  1. Leukemia—Juvenile literature. I. Title. II. Series: Health alert
(Benchmark Books)

  RC643.K66 2005
  616.99'419—dc22   2005005002

Front cover: Red and white blood cells from a leukemia patient
Title page: Red blood cells and leukemia cells

Photo research by Candlepants, Inc.
Front cover: SPL / Photo Researchers, Inc.
The photographs in this book are used by permission and through the courtesy of: *Photo Researchers, Inc:* Philippa Uwins, Whistler Research Pty., 11; Carlyn Iverson, 15; Nibsc, 17; Michael Gilles, 18; SPL, 20; Prof. Aaron Polliack, 23; Kenneth Edward, 25; Geoff Tompkinson, 28; John Bavosi, 31; Novosti, 35; James King-Holmes, 39; LADA / Hop Americain, 41; Simon Fraser, 48; Science Source, 51. *Science Photo Library / Photo Researchers, Inc.:* Alfred Pasieka, 13; Colin Cuthbert, 46; Simon Fraser, 54. *Corbis:* 43; Bettmann, 33; Philip James Corwin, 36. *K.D.:* 8, 55.

Printed in China
6 5 4 3 2 1

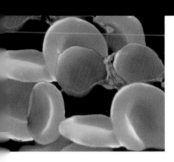

CONTENTS

1

WHAT IS IT LIKE TO HAVE LEUKEMIA?

Kayla was a little over two years old when her parents learned that she had leukemia. They had not noticed anything unusual about her, until a worker at Kayla's daycare called one day to say she was a little pale and just did not seem well. So her parents picked Kayla up and took her to the doctor. The doctor checked her over and took a sample of her blood. He discovered she had signs of leukemia. Kayla went to the hospital right away, where other tests were done. When the test results came in they found out that Kayla had ALL (Acute Lymphocytic Leukemia), the most common type of leukemia that children develop.

"We were lucky to catch it so early," her dad recalls. "So

treatment began right away. She did not become as sick as some kids do before anyone realizes they have leukemia. The earlier the treatment starts, the better chance they will work."

The treatments did work for Kayla, but they were not easy. For a little more than two years she took many different kinds of medication. She would take them every day for a couple of weeks, then stop for a while to let her body rest. Some of the medication could be swallowed, while others had to be injected into her body.

The medication caused a lot of changes in Kayla's body. As is common for people undergoing leukemia treatments, Kayla's hair fell out. Also, her weight went up and down as she went on and off the medication. During Kayla's years of treatment, doctors were constantly watching out for **infections** and problems that the medication can cause. Kayla had to come into the hospital once because of an infection, but luckily, she got better.

During her treatments, Kayla and her family were helped by many leukemia organizations. These organizations focus on helping children—and their families—who are dealing

Leukemia treatments did not stop Kayla from doing fun things like enjoying the outdoors.

with diseases such as leukemia. They also provide a support system for the children and their families. Many people find comfort in being in touch with others who are undergoing similar experiences. These charitable organizations often sponsor programs for children to attend. The programs provide activities and other fun opportunities for children who are ill or undergoing treatment. One example is a summer camp for children who have leukemia. Kayla spent a summer at this camp and took part in activities like hiking and playing outdoors.

Fortunately, Kayla's leukemia treatments worked. And today—years after she finished leukemia treatments—Kayla is healthy, active and happy. She goes to school and participates in activities just like other kids her age. She is even part of a soccer team. But Kayla will still go for a check-up at the doctor's every year until she is eighteen, just to be sure the disease has not returned.

Kayla was lucky that her parents and doctors discovered the disease early and were able to start treatments. Kayla's family lived near a very good children's hospital and they were especially happy with how pleasant and helpful the doctors and nurses were, and how great a place the hospital was for kids.

"Years ago kids who got this disease did not have much of a chance," says Kayla's dad. "That has changed with newer treatments, and doctors are continually looking for ways to improve them. Kayla's success story is one of the best medical stories there is."

2

WHAT IS LEUKEMIA?

Leukemia is a disease in which a group of cells that are normally found in the bloodstream become so plentiful that they endanger a person's life. Some people talk about leukemia as a **cancer** of blood cells, but others say it is different enough from cancer that the comparison is not helpful. To understand leukemia, it is helpful to first know some things about how our bodies work when they are healthy.

A TRILLION CELLS

Our bodies are made of trillions of tiny living things called cells. They are too small to be seen without using a microscope. There are many kinds of cells, which group together to form different parts of our bodies. For example, cells that make up our skin are different from those of our muscles. Even bones have cells in them. Some things like hair, fingernails, and the outer surface of your skin are made of cells that have died but are packed together and are still clinging to the body.

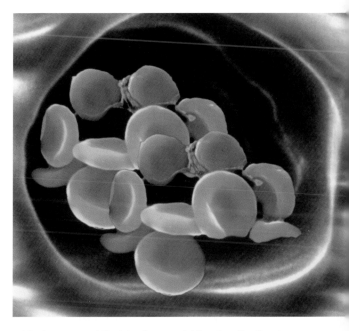

This is a magnified look at red blood cells flowing through a blood vessel.

The living cells in our bodies constantly need **nutrients,** water, and oxygen to stay alive. That is why we eat meals and snacks, drink beverages, and are constantly breathing air into our lungs. But how can the foods and beverages that we digest get to all the cells in our body? And how does oxygen in the air get from our lungs to cells in places like our toes? We have blood to thank for that.

BLOOD

You have probably noticed that there are blue-colored lines just under the skin of your wrists, hands, or in other places. Those are some of your blood vessels. Blood vessels are tubes that carry blood to every living cell in the body. Blood is a reddish liquid that is continually pushed through the vessels by the pumping action of the heart. Nearly everyone has seen blood by the time they are a couple of years old, because blood vessels often break or are torn when a person gets hurt. Almost everyone who has scraped a knee or an elbow has seen a little blood.

Blood is an amazing thing. It carries important materials—like the nutrients from the food you have eaten and oxygen that entered your lungs—to cells in every nook and cranny of your body. Sometimes a doctor or nurse will take a small sample of a person's blood to be sure that it has all the right things in it.

One thing blood should have is the right kind and number of cells. Even though blood looks like a red liquid, about half of it is made of cells. The other half is made of a pale yellow liquid called plasma. Learning more about the cells in blood will make it easier to understand leukemia.

Red Blood Cells

The most obvious kind of cell in the blood is a **red blood cell,** or RBC for short. There are about 4 to 6 million RBCs in a cubic millimeter of blood. (A cubic millimeter of blood is about the size of a small drop.) RBCs are packed full of a reddish substance called **hemoglobin.** Hemoglobin gives blood its red color. Hemoglobin can also attach to oxygen. So when RBCs travel through blood vessels in the lungs, their hemoglobin grabs a lot of oxygen from the air inside the lungs. Later, when those same RBCs travel through blood vessels in some other part of the body, the hemoglobin releases the oxygen to cells that need it.

If there are not enough RBCs in a person's blood, or if they do not have enough hemoglobin in them, they cannot carry enough oxygen for all the body's cells. This condition is called **anemia.** Without enough oxygen, a person's muscle cells cannot work very long before they tire. Brain cells will not work well, either, and a person may feel dizzy, faint, or confused.

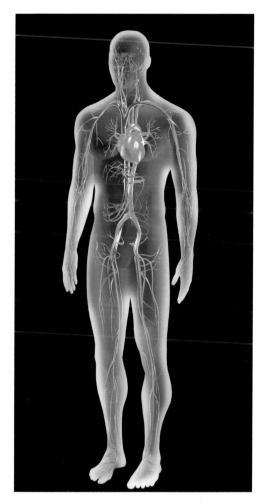

The circulatory system distributes blood (and the nutrients it carries) through a system of vessels spanning nearly all parts of the human body.

Low oxygen levels mean that heart cells cannot push blood through the vessels as forcefully. This could be a problem, because in order to survive, a person needs his or her heart to pump oxygenated (oxygen-rich) blood throughout the body. Sometimes, when cells do not get enough oxygen they die, and that can cause a person to die, too. Most cases of anemia can be treated with special medication or nutritional supplements.

White Blood Cells

Blood contains other cells besides RBCs. These are called **white blood cells,** or WBCs for short. They are much less numerous than RBCs, with only about 4,000 to 11,000 WBCs in a cubic millimeter of blood. WBCs are not red because they do not have hemoglobin in them. When many WBCs are collected together they look white.

Not all WBCs are the same. Some have tiny specks in them that sparkle when colored dyes are added. The specks are called granules, and the WBCs that have them are called **granulocytes** (*cyte* means "cell"). There are a few different types of granulocytes found in the human body. Scientists now know that the different granulocytes each have a different way to help a person fight off infections. The granules contain chemicals that help each white blood cell do its own particular job.

There are also white blood cells that do not have granules. These are sometimes called agranulocytes (the *a* means "without"). Some of these are called **lymphocytes.** There are B-lymphocytes and T-lympho-cytes—these are called **B-cells** and **T-cells.** Both types help fight off **pathogens,** which are **bacteria, viruses,** parasites, and other things that can cause disease. Pathogens are what make us sick with infections or illness like colds and the flu.

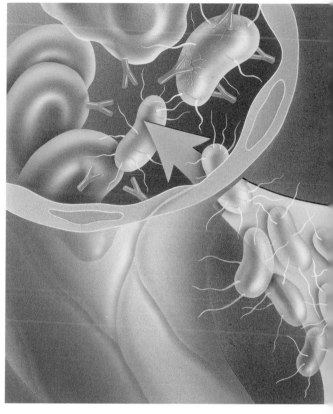

This illustration shows part of the immune system at work. Bacteria (shown as hairy-looking structures) have entered the bloodstream. Antibodies (represented as Y-shaped objects) attach themselves to the bacteria. These markers tell other immune cells to kill the bacteria.

B-cells help fight off pathogens by making **antibodies.** Antibodies are substances that stick to the pathogen's surface, and act like a flag that says, "This is a dangerous invader!" Then other types of white blood cells come along and destroy the flagged pathogen.

T-cells also help keep the body free of infection, but in very different ways. Some make chemicals that improve the ability of B-cells, T-cells, and other white blood cells to fight invading pathogens. Other T-cells destroy the body's own

Memory Cells

....

There are special T-cells and B-cells called memory cells. These cells remember the different pathogens that they have fought off before. That way, the next time the same pathogens enter the body, the cells know that they need to attack and destroy them. Memory cells allow the body to quickly and successfully prevent—or at least limit— the spread of an infection or other illness.

cells if they have become infected. Doing so helps to keep the infecting pathogen from spreading to other cells.

A natural killer cell is another type of white blood cell. It is something like a T-cell. Natural killer cells destroy cells in the body that have **mutated**. Mutated cells no longer behave normally. They are not pathogens, because they are part of a person's own body, but mutated cells can be very dangerous. If some escape being noticed by natural killer cells and are not destroyed, they can cause serious diseases like cancer. Leukemia is caused by mutated cells.

Another type of white blood cell is a **macrophage.** These cells are like the garbage collectors and recyclers of the body. Their name means "big eater" (*macro-* means "large" and *phage* means "eat"). They are especially good at grabbing pathogens and destroying them. They also clean up dead cells. They do this by surrounding a pathogen or cell and breaking it down into tiny bits that can be reused by healthy cells. This process is called **phagocytosis**. Macrophages live in all parts of the body, but they can be found in an early stage of their lives in the blood, with other white blood cells. There, they are called **monocytes.**

To summarize, white blood cells work together to keep a person free of infections and illnesses. They are like a team of guards that are always on the lookout for pathogens or mutated cells. When they find something in the body that is not right they work together to destroy it. All these cells and their activities are a part of the **immune system.**

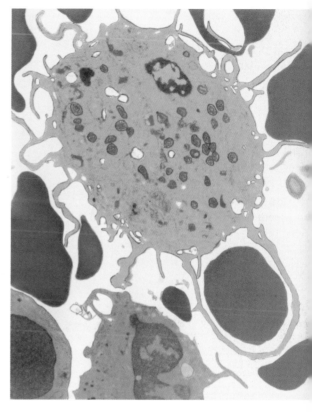

Phagocytosis is what some immune cells do to invaders. They encircle the invader (shown here where the yellow "arm" closes around the red invader) and then destroy or digest it.

BONE MARROW

Leukemia also involves the bones. Bones are strong and hard, which makes them an excellent material with which to build a skeleton. But most bones have a soft inner core called **marrow.** Blood cells are made in bone marrow.

Blood cells do not live as long as you do and need to be

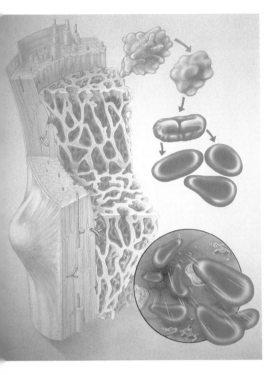

This illustration shows how our bones have hollow spaces filled with stem cells that produce RBCs and WBCs.

replaced constantly. Red blood cells live for about four months before they fall apart due to the wear and tear of squeezing through blood vessels. White blood cells need to be replaced too, though some live for years. Blood cell production is also important because when a person has an infection, millions of white blood cells need to be made to carry out the fight.

The new RBCs and WBCs are made in bone marrow, by a group of cells called **stem cells.** Stem cells are constantly multiplying, making new cells. Some of the stem cells in the marrow develop into RBCs, which leave the marrow to carry out their duty in the bloodstream. Others become new WBCs—including granulocytes, lymphocytes, and monocytes. So there are always developing RBCs and WBCs in bone marrow.

After these WBCs develop in the marrow, they travel to other parts of the body. As a result, adults have WBCs in the spleen (an organ that stores many WBCs and helps recycle old RBCs), tonsils (small organs far back in the throat), intestines (a part of the digestive system), liver (an organ that helps remove pathogens and toxins from the blood), skin, brain, and lymph nodes. Lymph nodes are small, roundish lumps (usually the size of a pea or kidney bean) found in the armpit, neck, groin, and many other locations. In all these places, and in the bloodstream and bone marrow as well, WBCs are "on guard" for invading pathogens.

WHAT GOES WRONG

Imagine what would happen if a person's WBCs stopped doing their jobs. Pathogens that get into the body would go unnoticed and start infections. Without the WBCs to rid the body of these invaders, a person would become very sick, and might even die.

In leukemia, WBCs are not doing their jobs. In fact, a common way a person finds out that she or he has leukemia is by going to the doctor because of an infection that will not go away. But, a blood sample of a person with leukemia usually shows that they have plenty of WBCs around—in fact, far too many! So what is going on? How can a person have so many white blood cells, but cannot fight off infections?

In most cases of leukemia, it appears that a single WBC is the culprit. Somewhere in bone marrow, a WBC becomes

An enlarged view of leukemia cells (purple) crowding out red blood cells. Normlly, red blood cells are the most numerous cells in the blood.

mutated. In leukemia, the mutated cell is somehow able to avoid being destroyed by natural killer cells. So it survives. It also starts making copies of itself, and each copy is mutated. The mutated cells make more copies. Together, all these copies of a single cell are called a **clone.**

A clone of mutated WBCs may not seem dangerous, but there are two problems at work. One is that these mutated cells, which can also be called leukemia cells, do not function properly as WBCs. Some do not do their jobs at all. So they are useless as protectors against infection.

The other problem is that the mutated cells multiply into such a huge group that they crowd the bone marrow, flood the bloodstream, and collect in body organs and other places. The mutated cells use up nutrients, oxygen, and space that are needed by normal cells. Without these things, stem cells cannot make as many RBCs or normal WBCs as a person needs. Without enough RBCs, a person can suffer from anemia. Without enough WBCs, the immune system becomes weaker and weaker. Pathogens take hold and infections occur. If the clone is not stopped, the person may die.

WHAT CAUSES A MUTATION?

Billions of dollars and decades of scientific research have been devoted to discovering what causes a cell to become mutated and change into a dangerous leukemia-causing cell. Scientists have some answers, although many mysteries remain.

Four things are known to increase the likelihood of a mutation in a person's cells. One is exposure to the chemical benzene. It had been used as a cleaner in factories, until it was banned for that purpose in 1977. But it is still used, and hundreds of thousands of workers in the United States may be exposed to benzene doing jobs like making plastic and rubber products, working with gasoline and petroleum, printing, shoemaking, and steel manufacturing. Statistics have shown that these factory workers tend to develop leukemia more often than other people.

Benzene also evaporates easily and can get into the air

from products in our houses and buildings. Some of these products include glues, paints, furniture wax, and detergents. Studies have shown that benzene is also present in tobacco smoke. Benzene also enters the air when gasoline is burned as fuel for cars. A study in 2004 found that children who lived near gas stations developed leukemia far more often than other children did, possibly due to the benzene in the air.

The second thing that causes mutations in cells is dangerous radiation exposure. Radiation is energy that is released as waves or tiny particles. We are exposed to low levels of radiation every day. The Sun's rays contain different types of radiation. X-ray machines, microwaves, and other similar machines release small amounts of radiation that do not cause serious harm.

But people can be exposed to dangerously high levels of radiation if there is an explosion or accident at a **nuclear** power plant. Certain types of bombs also contain high amounts of radiation. Many instances of leukemia were caused by these radiation sources.

Some illnesses, like cancer, are treated with large amounts of radiation. The radiation is used to kill cancer cells to stop the disease. While the radiation often helps to treat the cancer, studies have shown that cancer patients who were treated with radiation are more likely to get leukemia years later.

A third cause of cell mutations that can lead to leukemia is **chemotherapy.** Chemotherapy is a cancer treatment that uses strong medication to kill cancer cells. As with radiation, patients with cancer who have been treated with chemotherapy have an increased chance of developing leukemia.

A fourth thing that causes mutations, especially in T-cells, is a virus known as human T-cell lymphotropic virus, type one (HTLV-I). Fortunately, the

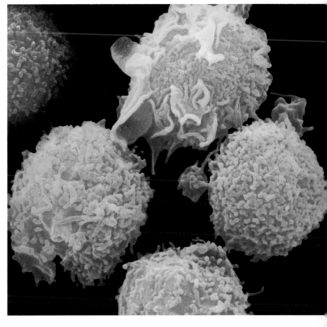

This magnified scan has been colorized to show the distinctive features of white blood cells affected by hairy cell leukemia. The hairlike projections and ruffles (shown in pink) on the outside of the cells indicate that these are mutated white blood cells.

virus is not easily spread among people. It must be passed when a person comes into contact with infected blood. Fewer than 5 percent of people who are infected with the virus get leukemia, and symptoms—or signs of the disease—usually do not show up for decades.

There are probably other causes of mutations that just have not yet been identified. Scientists believe that other chemicals besides benzene might lead to leukemia. Formaldehyde is one of them, and traces of it are present in products made of plastic or other man-made materials, including some carpets. The fact that many cases of leukemia are unexplained leads some people to choose products that have as few man-made chemicals in them as possible, and to eat foods without added chemicals like pesticides.

SYMPTOMS OF LEUKEMIA

A person often first learns he or she has leukemia because symptoms of the disease start to appear. A common symptom of leukemia is frequent and serious infections that will not go away. That happens because the white blood cells are not working well enough to rid the body of pathogens.

Another symptom of leukemia is **fatigue**, which means feeling very tired and weak. Healthy people experience fatigue after getting a lot of exercise, but for someone with leukemia, fatigue happens without a lot of physical activity. Both of these symptoms—infection and fatigue—happen because the clone of leukemia cells is preventing the body from making enough normal white and red blood cells.

Another symptom of leukemia is bruising often and easily. When you injure yourself, for example, when you bump your arm hard against something, you usually end up with a bruise—a red or purplish area beneath your skin. The bruise is a result of blood leaking out of blood vessels that have been torn or broken. When you cut yourself on something, you also bleed because blood vessels have been damaged. People with leukemia get bruises very often and very easily. When they cut or scrape themselves, people with leukemia tend to bleed a lot—and it takes a long time before the bleeding stops.

For people with leukemia, the symptoms of bruising easily and bleeding a lot when cut or scraped are due to a shortage of **platelets** in the bloodstream. In a healthy person, platelets stop blood from escaping out of a torn or broken blood vessel by collecting in a sticky clump, called a blood clot. This clot clogs up the leaking vessel. Platelets are present in blood all the time, ready to form a clot when needed.

Platelets are made in bone marrow, by cells called **megakaryocytes.** Megakaryocytes have the unusual job of growing to a large size and then breaking into pieces—the pieces are the platelets. All through a person's

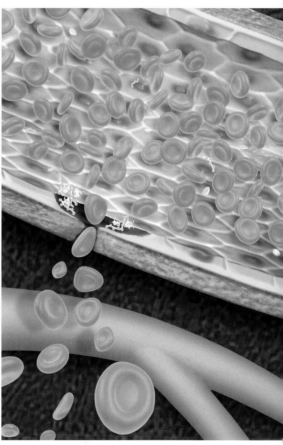

When a blood vessel breaks, platelets (yellow and blue structures) are supposed to gather at the injury site to seal the break and promote healing.

Leukemia and Lymphoma

....

A kind of disease that is very much related to leukemia is lymphoma. Lymphoma is named for lymph nodes, because the symptoms of the disease include enlarged lymph nodes. Lymph nodes are home to several kinds of white blood cells. In lymphoma, a clone of mutated white blood cells is taking over and multiplying out of control.

Some doctors think of lymphoma as different from leukemia, because the bone marrow may look normal in lymphoma. But studies have convinced other doctors that the two diseases have so much in common that they may just be different stages of the same problem. For example, some people with lymphoma eventually develop bone marrow problems like that of leukemia.

As with leukemia, there are different kinds of lymphoma. The two main categories are Hodgkin's lymphoma, in which a specific type of mutated cell is present, and NonHodgkin's lymphomas, which includes all the other forms. Lymphoma is treated the same way as leukemia, using chemotherapy, radiation, and bone marrow transplantation, although treatment of smaller areas of the body (around diseased lymph nodes) may be possible.

life, megakaryocytes are self-destructing to provide the blood with platelets, while new megakaryoctyes are being created from stem cells in the marrow. But leukemia cells crowd out megakaryocytes, and platelets become scarce. Because they cannot form blood clots quickly, people with leukemia have to be very careful about getting injured.

There are other symptoms of leukemia, too, such as fever, bone pain, headaches, night sweats (very uncomfortable, heavy sweating while sleeping), and a lack of appetite. But all of the symptoms mentioned here can also be caused by diseases other than leukemia. It is important for a doctor to run special tests to determine whether or not a person has leukemia or some other illness.

TYPES OF LEUKEMIA

Once it is determined that a person has leukemia, it is important to find out what kind of leukemia he or she has. There are several types of leukemia, because there are many kinds of white blood cells and a variety of mutations that can happen to those cells. Within each of these types of leukemia are subtypes—more specific types. Knowing what type and subtype a leukemia patient has will help a doctor plan a course of treatment. Because the names of these types of leukemia are complicated, it will help to first understand some words used in them:

Acute. This means that a person's symptoms become serious very quickly, and the leukemia cells are reproducing rapidly. Without medical treatment, a person with acute leukemia can die in less than six months.

Chronic. This means the disease is progressing slowly. Leukemia cells are not so plentiful and are still doing their jobs pretty well. A person with a chronic type of leukemia may not need treatment right away. Instead, doctors watch and wait, and only begin treatment when symptoms get bad or leukemia cells become more abundant.

Other words used to name leukemia describe the cells that are abnormal. If they resemble lymphocytes, *lympho-* will be in the name. If they do not, then the name will have *granulo-*, for granulocytes, or *myelo-*, which actually means "marrow," but has come to refer to the group of white blood cells that are not lymphocytes.

Acute Lymphocytic Leukemia (ALL)

ALL is the most common type of leukemia among young people. It is also known as acute lymphoid leukemia and acute lymphoblastic leukemia. About 85 percent of people with ALL have a clone of leukemia cells that are like B-cells and 15 percent of people with ALL have a T-cell clone.

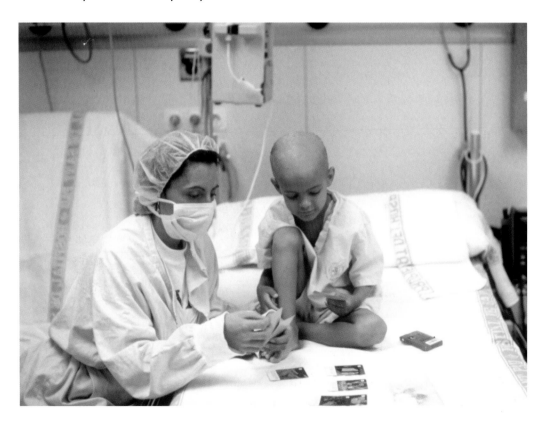

A young leukemia patient plays cards with his mother at the hospital. The child is undergoing leukemia treatments for ALL, which is why he has no hair.

Each year in the United States, about 2,400 children under the age of 20 and about 1,000 adults are found to have ALL. Some infants are born with mutated cells that are thought to later cause ALL. Doctors suspect that a pregnant woman's exposure to radiation might cause the mutation in the developing infant. Most often, though, symptoms first show up when a person is about two or three years old.

Acute Myelogenous Leukemia (AML)

About 12,000 people a year find out they have AML. Most of them are over 40 years of age, although about 25 percent of children who get leukemia have this type. Other names for AML are acute myelocytic leukemia, acute myeloblastic leukemia, acute granulocytic leukemia, and acute nonlymphocytic leukemia. AML is a grouping of many different forms of leukemia. What these forms have in common is that the leukemia cells are not lymphocytes. Some forms of AML have leukemia cells that look like granulocytes. In another form, they appear to be monocytes. One type of AML has leukemia cells that appear to be poorly formed red blood cells. Another form of AML has cells like the ones that make platelets. And in some cases, the cells are so immature that their identity is hard to determine. Like ALL, AML is caused by exposure to radiation or to chemicals like benzene.

Chronic Lymphocytic Leukemia, (CLL)

About 8,000 people in the United States learn that they have CLL each year. It is extremely rare in children, and nearly everyone who gets CLL is at least fifty years old. Another name for the disease is chronic lymphoid leukemia. Almost always, the leukemia cells are like B-cells, not T-cells. Unlike the other three major types of leukemia, there is no evidence that CLL is caused by exposure to benzene or radiation. The human T-cell lymphotropic virus, type one (HTLV-I) causes some forms of CLL.

Chronic Myelogenous Leukemia (CML)

In the United States, over 4,000 people get CML each year. Most of them are adults. CML is also called chronic granulocytic, chronic myelocytic, or chronic myeloid leukemia. This form of leukemia is a slow accumulation of cells that look like granulocytes. Almost everyone with CML has the same type of cell mutation. Scientists have figured out that the mutation makes an abnormal chemical that causes the leukemia cells to multiply. Fortunately, scientists have been able to create a new medication that seems to be working very well to destroy those cells.

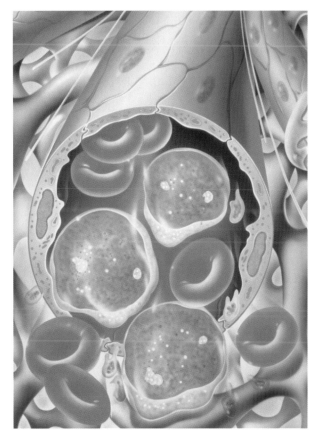

Finding large, immature white blood cells (shown in pink with white borders) in the bloodstream is a sign of leukemia.

There are still mysteries about leukemia, but new discoveries are being made all the time. Progress in research, and new tools and technologies in use today are helping to solve the remaining mysteries.

3

THE HISTORY OF LEUKEMIA

The word *leukemia* means "white blood." The blood of a leukemia patient still looks red because of the red blood cells, but a closer look, using a microscope, reveals many more white blood cells than normal. Though scientists believe that the disease has existed for thousands of years, leukemia was first described in the 1840s by a German doctor and teacher named Rudolf Ludwig Karl Virchow.

During Dr. Virchow's time, not much was known about the causes of different illnesses. Most doctors thought that a sickness indicated that the whole body was diseased. But Dr. Virchow had the new idea that people become sick because something goes wrong with just some of their cells. He also believed that "every cell originates from another cell." Today we now know that both of Virchow's ideas are correct.

About a hundred years ago, doctors and scientists realized

that leukemia could be divided into different types. They counted white blood cells in a drop of blood and observed details about their appearance, using a microscope. These observations helped doctors understand that leukemia is not just one disease that occurs in exactly the same way in every patient. They realized that different types of leukemia cells can be found in different people.

Scientific inventions and special laboratory equipment (also called technologies) were created throughout the 1900s. They have added greatly to our understanding of

A scientist uses a microscope to look at slides of cancer cells. This photograph was taken around 1936 at cancer research center in New York.

leukemia. For example, high-powered microscopes, called electron microscopes, make it possible to view cells with remarkable detail. Cells can now be kept alive in the laboratory and studied to see what makes them multiply, and what destroys them. Also, ways of finding mutations in a cell have been invented.

Because of these technologies, scientists understand even more about the white blood cells in leukemia. Researchers found out that some leukemia cells that look alike really are not alike at all. Some have special substances on their surfaces, which can be marked with dyes that make them noticeable. That helps doctors know what kind of white blood cell made the clone. Sometimes they discover that more than one clone is present in the same leukemia patient. Knowing this helps doctors decide what treatment is best.

As technology improves, treatments for the disease also improve. Doctors continue to search for new ways to make leukemia treatment easier for the patient.

BOMBS, EXPLOSIONS, AND CANCER CLUSTERS

Unfortunately, the progress scientists are making with leukemia research is partly due to the increasing number of people with the disease. Events in the last few decades have also made scientists—and the public—more aware of leukemia and its effects. For example, in 1945, when the United States and other countries were at war with Japan during World War II, U.S. troops dropped a very destructive and dangerous bomb, called an **atomic bomb**, on a Japanese city named Hiroshima. Atomic bombs release very dangerous amounts of radiation. As a result, many of the people in or near Hiroshima died or developed serious illnesses, including leukemia.

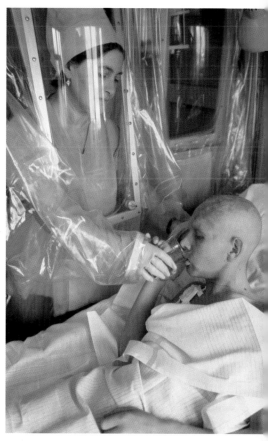

Another example of an unfortunate event that furthers scientific knowledge of diseases like leukemia occurred in 1986. An accidental explosion at a nuclear power plant in Chernobyl, located in part of the former Soviet Union, caused massive amounts of radiation to be released. Many people died and several were injured. A large number of Chernobyl residents developed diseases like leukemia and cancer. Winds also carried radioactive dust eastward, especially into Turkey, where leukemia has since

A nurse helps a Chernobyl survivor. This man suffers from radiation exposure.

A Thousand Peace Cranes

In 1945, Sadako Sasaki was a two-year-old girl living in Hiroshima when the atomic bomb was dropped. Sadako survived the blast, but she was one of the many people who became ill years later. In 1954, when she was eleven, Sadako was diagnosed with leukemia. A friend told her about a Japanese legend which said that if a person made 1,000 cranes (a type of bird much respected in Japan) out of folded paper, he or she would be granted a wish. Sadako wanted to get better, so she began to create the paper cranes.

Despite her illness and her weakening body, Sadako was able to make more than 1,000 cranes before she died in 1955 at the age of twelve. Sadako's strength touched the heart of many people. Her story was told around the world and as of today, many statues, monuments, and parks have been created to honor Sadako's story. The paper crane has since come to represent the wish for world peace.

A statue covered in colorful paper cranes.

become twelve times more common than it used to be.

There are neighborhoods in the country where many people have developed leukemia and other cancers. There is a great deal of concern and debate about these neighborhoods, which are called "cancer clusters." In the early 1980s, over two dozen people in the town of Woburn, Massachusetts, came down with leukemia. Chemical waste and other pollutants were secretly being dumped into the ground and water by a nearby plant. The people believed this polluted water caused the cases of leukemia and sued the plant. The story was made into a book and into a movie, both called *A Civil Action*.

Another example was in Fallon, Nevada, where nineteen children developed leukemia. Since 1997, three of those children have died. Jet fuel carried in underground pipes was suggested to be the cause, but no pipes appear to have been leaking. Studies have found high levels of arsenic, antimony, tungsten, cobalt, and uranium (different types of chemical elements) in Fallon, but their relation to the leukemia cases is not clear yet. Mark Witten, a research professor at the University of Arizona College of Medicine, is trying to find an answer for this and for the several leukemia cases that have appeared in Sierra Vista, Arizona, which also has jet fuel pipes underground.

There are other cancer clusters around the country, as well. The United States government is doing some studies on them, but many families with sick children want more action to be taken—and sooner. Some families hire researchers and lawyers to get more studies underway.

HOPE FOR THE FUTURE

There continues to be a great deal of research going on to better understand what causes leukemia and how to treat it. There are some hospitals and research centers that are devoted to research and treatment of people with leukemia and other cancers. Also, a great deal of money continues to be donated by people who want to help find cures for diseases like these. This helps pay for the expensive kinds of research needed to make new discoveries.

New discoveries have helped to improve the lives of many leukemia sufferers. For example, in 1962, few people survived the disease. Only 4 percent of children with ALL lived very long. But by the early 1970s, 50 percent of patients with ALL lived at least five years. Today, 75 to 85 percent of children remain free of symptoms for at least five years after treatment.

Many things have made this possible. Doctors and nurses now have lots of experience in taking care of leukemia patients. They can tell whether someone has the disease much more easily than they used to, which means that treatment can get underway sooner.

Many different medications exist to kill the leukemia cells, and many new ones are being tried. Other medications have been created to help patients deal with the harsh effects that treatments have on their bodies. Perhaps someday better treatments—and maybe even a cure—can be found.

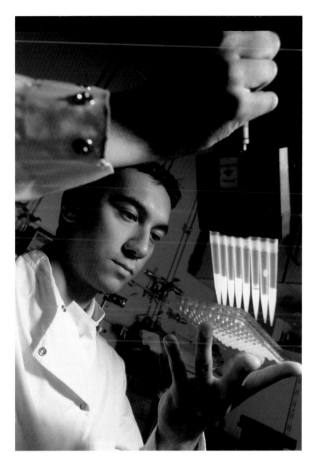

Newer technologies and scientific discoveries may one day help people find a cure for diseases like leukemia.

4

DIAGNOSING, TREATING, AND COPING WITH LEUKEMIA

Many tests and studies are needed to be certain a person has leukemia. Often, it starts with a physical exam by a doctor. A person might come in to see the doctor because he or she feels unusually tired for a long time, or because he or she has had many infections such as colds, the flu, bronchitis, sore throats, ear infections, and skin infections. The doctor will do a physical exam to check all areas of the body for signs of disease or anything unusual. Many questions will be asked about the person's health and habits, and the health of family members. The answers are important in deciding whether a person might be at risk of developing leukemia.

Studying a blood sample is essential in deciding if a person has leukemia. A doctor, nurse, or technician uses a syringe to draw blood—usually from a person's arm. The blood is sent to a lab where it is analyzed. One thing that is checked is the number of red and white blood cells in the blood. This is often called a white blood cell count. A very high white blood cell count is common in people with leukemia.

The blood cells are also examined under a microscope. If odd-looking white blood cells are found in a person's blood, the cells are studied in greater detail. A test called a cytogenetic analysis compares traits of the odd white blood cells to traits of normal white blood cells. Another study, called immunophenotyping, helps figure out exactly what kind of white blood cell started the leukemia clone.

A laboratory technician studies a blood sample with a microscope and counts white blood cells.

If a doctor thinks that a person may have leukemia, a sample of bone marrow will be studied next. This is important because some people with leukemia have a normal number of white blood cells in their blood. Others have normal-looking white blood cells in the blood. Testing the marrow will provide the doctors with more information.

The procedure involved in taking a sample of bone marrow is called a marrow biopsy or marrow aspiration. To take a marrow sample, a doctor uses a long needle to withdraw a small portion of marrow from a patient's hipbone or breastbone. These bones are chosen because they are close to the skin and are easier to get to. Other bones, such as leg bones are surrounded by thicker muscles so getting marrow from there would be more difficult and more painful.

The sample is examined under powerful microscopes. Doctors look at these living cells to count the number of white blood cells present in the marrow. Examining the sample also shows what the white blood cells look like, and how they are packed together with other types of cells in the marrow.

Besides blood tests and marrow biopsies, a doctor might use special imaging machines to see inside a person's body. Sometimes a chest X ray is used. This is a fast and painless way to get a picture of the inside of a person's upper body. A CT scan (sometimes called a CAT scan or a computed axial tomography scan) is another painless way that a doctor can get very detailed pictures of internal organs. With X rays and CT scans, doctors are looking at the sizes and shapes of organs such as the liver, spleen, or lymph nodes. These structures might be enlarged or strangely shaped if large amounts of leukemia cells are gathering there.

A CT scan machine is shaped like a tunnel, inside which a patient rests laying down. Within the tunnel is the special imaging equipment that takes detailed pictures of a person's internal organs.

To test for leukemia, it is also common to sample the fluid that surrounds the brain and spinal cord. This fluid is called cerebrospinal fluid (CSF). Doctors use medication to numb the skin and then, using a needle, draw fluid from the spine at different spots on a person's lower back. If mutated white blood cells are found in the CSF, the patient will get treatments that are especially meant to kill white blood cells in the brain and spinal cord.

TREATMENTS FOR LEUKEMIA

Once a doctor has decided a person has leukemia, a decision will be made about what treatment is best. If the leukemia is an acute type, the white blood cell count is usually very high, and treatment must begin right away. If it is a chronic type, the doctor may choose to "watch and wait" for months or years until treatment becomes necessary.

The type of treatment each patient receives and the length of the treatment are decided by a doctor who is an expert in leukemia. The goal in leukemia treatment is to get rid of all the leukemia cells, wherever they may be. This is a challenge, because there can be millions of them in different parts of the body. So the treatments must be strong. Unfortunately, during treatment many healthy cells are killed along with leukemia cells.

Acute leukemia (or chronic leukemia that has become more serious) is treated in phases or stages. The first phase is called induction therapy. Its purpose is to kill all leukemia cells in the blood and bone marrow. During induction therapy, blood samples and a marrow sample are checked to see if the mutated white blood cells are gone. If not, more treatments are done. When no signs of the leukemia cells remain, the patient is said to be in **remission.**

Most children and many adults reach remission after induction therapy. But doctors have learned over the years that a few mutated white blood cells may linger in hidden places. Over time they can multiply into a large group of leukemia cells once again. When that happens, it is called **recurrence,** and a second treatment phase is done. It is called consolidation therapy or consolidation/intensification therapy. Some patients will receive a third phase of leukemia treatment, called maintenance therapy (also called continuation therapy), to be sure no new leukemia cells come back. This phase is not usually done for children with AML because the other phases of treatment are very strong.

Depending upon the type of leukemia, some patients will also need treatment called intrathecal chemotherapy or CNS sanctuary therapy. (CNS stands for central nervous system, meaning the brain and spinal cord.) This therapy is done to make sure that any leukemia cells in the CNS are killed. This is especially true for patients with ALL, because it is very common for that kind of leukemia to spread to the CNS.

Chemotherapy

Chemotherapy, or "chemo" for short, uses medication to kill cells that are multiplying rapidly. (Leukemia cells and cancer cells tend to multiply *very* quickly.) A couple of different medications are used together, although sometimes just one is used. The patient usually takes a dose of the medication and then has a brief period where he or she will not take it. This allows the body to recover from any effects of the medication. These two steps—taking the medication and then recovering—are called a treatment cycle. The number of cycles a patient goes through depends on how well the medications are working, and how the patient is feeling.

There are a few different ways chemotherapy medication can be given. Some types can simply be swallowed. But the stomach's digestive actions interfere with other types. If that is the case, then the medication is injected directly into a person's bloodstream. This can be done in two ways. One method is **intravenous,** or IV, in which the medications are injected into a vein using a needle. The other is to put the medications into a **catheter.** A catheter is a thin, flexible tube that can be used to get liquids in or out of a person's body. For chemotherapy, a doctor inserts a catheter into the patient's vein (usually in the upper chest) and leaves it there for as long as a patient needs to take the medication. A small portion of the catheter sticks out above the skin, so that the medication can be put into it.

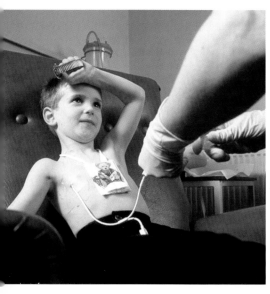

A young boy is given chemotherapy drugs through a catheter.

A recent addition to chemotherapy is a step called stem cell transplantation. In this procedure, healthy marrow stem cells are removed from another person and injected into a patient who has undergone chemotherapy. The stem cells travel to the patient's marrow, settle in, and provide a new supply of healthy red and white blood cells and megakaryocytes. This helps the patient recover more rapidly from the chemotherapy, which kills many of his or her marrow cells.

Some people come into a doctor's office or hospital for their chemotherapy and then go home. Other people stay at a hospital or in a special treatment center, so that they can be well cared for as their bodies deal with the very strong effects of the medication.

Radiation Therapy

A doctor may decide that a patient would do better with radiation therapy instead of, or in addition to, chemotherapy. Radiation therapy is also called radiotherapy, X-ray therapy, or irradiation. It is a painless procedure that only takes a few minutes. The patient lies down near a machine that produces radiation that is strong enough to pass into the body and damage or destroy the leukemia cells. Radiation therapy usually is given once a day for several days in a row, followed by a few days of rest. This is repeated for a few weeks.

Bone Marrow Transplantation

A doctor may decide that a patient has a better chance of getting rid of the leukemia cells with bone marrow transplantation (BMT). This procedure is used for people whose leukemia is progressing very quickly or for people who develop leukemia cells after remission. It is also the only reliable treatment, so far, for people with CML.

BMT is done in a hospital. It starts with radiation therapy that

Doctors use a large and long needle to withdraw—and replace—bone marrow.

is strong enough to kill leukemia cells in the marrow. But healthy cells die, too. In order to survive, the patient must be given new marrow cells from a donor (a person with healthy marrow). If all goes well, the leukemia cells have been destroyed, and the donated cells create new, healthy marrow for the patient. It usually takes several months for the patient to build up a new immune system from the donated marrow, however. During that period, the patient can easily develop infections, so he or she must be carefully watched by doctors and may need lots of medication to fight off illnesses. Also, the radiation itself can be very damaging to healthy tissue.

Unfortunately, some people do not survive the BMT procedure.

BMT is not an option for everyone. The donor's marrow must be very similar to the healthy cells of the leukemia patient, and sometimes a suitable donor is never found. Sometimes special drives or fundraisers are held to try to find someone who has bone marrow that can be used for transplantation.

If a donor is not found, doctors sometimes try something else. They can remove some of the patient's own marrow before the radiation step and keep it alive while the person undergoes radiation therapy. The marrow that was removed is then put back after the radiation treatment. Of course, any leukemia cells in the marrow must be destroyed before putting it back in the patient. This does not always work, but for some patients, it is the best chance for survival.

TREATMENT SIDE EFFECTS

Doctors and researchers are always looking for better ways to treat leukemia, because the treatments that are saving people's lives also have some serious side effects. Side effects are unpleasant or dangerous changes in the body that are caused by medication or treatment procedures like radiation therapy. Side effects happen because the chemotherapy and radiation kill some normal cells along with the leukemia cells. When these normal, healthy cells are killed, the body cannot function correctly.

A very common side effect of leukemia treatment is fatigue. This can last for weeks, as the body heals from the treatments and gets rid of damaged cells. It is important for people who are undergoing leukemia treatment to get plenty of rest. Many people find that a little bit of exercise—like short daily walks— can help. The amount and type of physical activity, however, should be determined by the person's doctor. Another common side effect is loss of appetite. It is important, though, that a person who is undergoing leukemia treatment eats a balanced diet. This will help the body recover. Patients who have no appetite learn a few tricks to eating right while going through this, such as eating small meals several times a day and making nutritious beverages that are easily swallowed.

Another common side effect is hair loss. Hair is actually made of millions of cells packed together. Chemotherapy and radiation kill cells that are multiplying rapidly and that includes cells that make hair. Usually the hair grows back after the treatments have stopped, although in some cases it does not.

A person undergoing leukemia treatments has very little immune system protection against illness, because chemotherapy and radiation destroy stem cells that are multiplying to make new, healthy white blood cells. So it is common for the patient to live in a special hospital for a while, where any infections can be treated immediately with medication. In addition, the leukemia treatments damage the marrow cells that make red blood cells and platelets. Fortunately, researchers are finding that some chemicals help the cells in bone marrow multiply and mature faster. One is called granulocyte colony-stimulating factor, and it does just what its name says. It stimulates granulocytes to make colonies (groups of cells) in bone marrow.

Doctors also know that leukemia treatment may cause

problems later on in life. In some cases, medication damages a patient's liver, kidneys, or heart. This may happen long after the treatment has ended and can become a life-threatening situation. People recovering from leukemia have regular check-ups so that doctors can monitor these kinds of problems.

When a person undergoes chemotherapy and other cancer treatments, the immune system is weakened. This often means that he or she must be separated from other people because it is too easy to catch a cold or develop some other illness.

Children who have received radiation therapy might not grow as tall as other children. However, some children are given a medication called growth hormone, which helps them to grow better and reach a normal height.

Chemotherapy or radiation treatment often affects a person's reproductive system (the body system responsible for having children.) Because of the damage to cells during treatment, many people who undergo these therapies cannot have children.

Another problem is that treatments can cause cancer to develop years later. This is because chemotherapy and radiation therapy can mutate healthy cells, which then become cancerous. Cataracts, which are a cloudiness that forms on the eye's clear surface, sometimes develop as a result of radiation therapy.

Since these side effects can be very difficult to go through, some people with leukemia wonder if treating the illness is worth it. But most people decide that the chance to survive leukemia is worth the discomfort and pain these treatments may cause. Also, these side effects do not necessarily affect every single person who undergoes leukemia treatment. But doctors keep a careful watch over how a patient looks and feels during each phase of therapy. If dangerous side effects begin, the doctor may change or end the treatments.

NEW TREATMENTS

Doctors and medical researchers are busily searching for new and better leukemia treatments that will still be effective, but not cause such bad side effects. Scientists are using some of the latest discoveries about mutated cells to design procedures that can kill the mutated cells without harming normal cells. These procedures are called targeted therapy, because they can hit a specific target—the leukemia cells—rather than damaging healthy cells as well. An example is a medication that prevents certain leukemia cells from making copies of themselves. The reason this works is because the exact mutation in some CML leukemia cells has been identified, and the medication "fixes" that mutation. Unfortunately, this may not work for other types of mutations, but it is a start.

Other new therapies are called biological therapies. These

therapies use what we know about how cells work to aid in the destruction of leukemia cells. For example, it is known that a person's immune system should be able to kill mutated cells, but leukemia cells somehow are not destroyed. So researchers are finding ways to get a patient's immune system to seek out and destroy leukemia cells. One way is by giving the patient antibodies that will attach to the leukemia cells and make them easier for white blood cells to notice and destroy. Another way is to give doses of chemicals to make the immune system more active. Many of those chemicals come from normal white blood cells like T-cells.

These and other new treatment ideas are very exciting. Some have side effects that can be dangerous, though, and others do not work very well. Some are just being studied, and it will be years before they are safe enough to test in real people. (So far these tests have been performed on cell samples and on laboratory animals.)

Some people with leukemia consider being part of a **clinical trial.** Clinical trials are studies of new combinations of medication, or of brand new therapies, which might become the treatments of the future. These clinical trials are often run at large health centers or research hospitals. Sometimes clinical trials are the last hope for people who are not responding to normal leukemia treatments.

COPING WITH LEUKEMIA

People with leukemia need more than medical treatment by a doctor. They need emotional support to endure years of testing and treatment. The support also helps them cope with the changes the disease makes in their social lives and the way the disease affects their schooling or careers. For people who have been treated, go into remission, but then develop leukemia again, the experience can be a rollercoaster of hopes and fears, successes and discouragement. Fortunately, there are many resources to draw upon for encouragement and support.

A number of treatment centers and hospitals around the country help leukemia patients deal with their feelings. Many have support groups where patients and their families can express their fears, make friends, and share ideas. These support groups have made it possible for some patients to continue battling their disease when they would have lost hope on their own.

Thanks to the Internet, people from a range of different places can support each other with online discussions about their disease. Patients who have

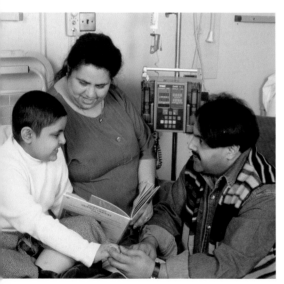

Family support is an important part of the healing process. This young girl has undergone leukemia treatments and, with the help of her parents, is getting better.

just been diagnosed can get advice and support from people who have made it through the disease. There is also an abundance of practical support for people with leukemia. For example, hospitals, doctor's offices, and the National Cancer Institute help people find ways to pay for treatment, because it is costly. There are also many booklets and Web sites that explain the disease and its treatments. Many people have found the Internet helpful when researching new discoveries and looking into clinical trials.

While there are still challenges to dealing with leukemia, treatments today are more effective than ever. There are many experts now, too, who have special understanding of the disease. As a result, children who find out they have leukemia very often go on to lead happy, normal lives.

Many children have survived leukemia. They go on to lead productive, happy, and healthy lives.

GLOSSARY

acute—A term used to describe some forms of leukemia in which symptoms get worse rapidly.

anemia—A condition of having too few red blood cells, or not enough hemoglobin within them, to carry enough oxygen to meet the body's needs. A person with anemia may feel weak, tired, dizzy, and confused.

antibodies—Substances produced by B-cells in response to a foreign substance in the body. They lock onto a foreign substance and help the body destroy or inactivate it.

atomic bomb—A bomb that gets its power from the energy and radiation released when atoms (the building blocks of all matter) are split. Also called a nuclear bomb.

B-cell—A type of lymphocyte that makes antibodies.

bacteria—Microscopic organisms composed of a single cell. Some are actually beneficial and live inside the body, others can cause illness.

cancer—A disease that involves fast-growing abnormal cells. Different types of cancers affect different body systems.

catheter—A thin, flexible tube that is used to give or remove liquids from a person's body.

chemotherapy—A kind of treatment for a disease, such as leukemia, that uses strong, cell-killing medication.

chronic—A term used to describe some forms of leukemia in which symptoms are slowly progressing.

clinical trial—A medical study that tests new medication or new ways of using existing medication.

clone—A group of identical cells. In leukemia, a single mutated white blood cell creates a clone of millions of cells just like itself, each with the same mutation.

diagnose—To determine whether or not a person has a certain illness.

fatigue—Extreme tiredness.

granulocyte—A type of white blood cell that has tiny specks (granules) in it, which are visible with a microscope.

hemoglobin—A reddish substance inside red blood cells. Oxygen attaches to hemoglobin and allows the cells to carry oxygen to all parts of the body.

immune system—The body system responsible for fighting off infections and diseases. Various organs and different types of cells make up this system.

infection—An illness caused by bacteria, viruses, parasites, or other pathogens that the immune system has not yet destroyed.

intravenous (IV)—A method of giving medication by using a needle or other device to inject medication into a vein.

lymphocyte—A type of white blood cell that does not have granules in it. B-cells and T-cells are the main types of lymphocytes, and are important parts of the body's immune system.

macrophage—A type of white blood cell that works with other white blood cells to destroy pathogens that have entered the body. Macrophages also get rid of dead or injured cells and "recycle" the useful bits.

marrow—The soft core found inside bones. Blood cells are made in the marrow.

megakaryocyte—A type of large cell in bone marrow that makes platelets.

monocyte—A white blood cell found in the blood which later becomes a macrophage.

mutate—To change a cell's genetic makeup, making the cell act abnormally.

nuclear—Having to do with energy that comes from splitting or combining atoms. Nuclear energy can be used in power plants or for bombs.

nutrients—Chemicals from digested foods that are needed for life and growth.

pathogen—Something that can cause disease or infection. Bacteria, viruses, and parasites are the most common pathogens.

phagocytosis—The process by which one cell engulfs a large particle or another cell. Macrophages use this process to destroy pathogens.

platelets—Small pieces of cells (megakaryocytes) that get into the blood and help blood to clot when a person is bleeding.

radiation—Energy that is released as waves or tiny particles.

recurrence—The return of a disease after it was thought to be gone.

red blood cells (RBCs)—Cells in the blood that carry oxygen. They are reddish in color because of the hemoglobin contained inside.

remission—A state in which there is no sign of disease.

stem cells—Cells that are continually dividing to make cells that can mature and carry out special tasks in the body. Stem cells in bone marrow usually become white or red blood cells.

T-cell—A type of lymphocyte.

virus— A microorganism that causes many diseases and illness in humans, animals, and plants.

white blood cells (WBCs)—Cells in the blood, bone marrow, lymph nodes, spleen, and elsewhere, which work together to fight off pathogens and to destroy infected cells in the body.

FIND OUT MORE

Organizations

The Leukemia and Lymphoma Society

1311 Mamaroneck Avenue

White Plains, New York 10605-5221

1-800-955-4572

http://www.leukemia-lymphoma.org

The National Children's Cancer Society

Suite 600

1015 Locust Street

Saint Louis, Missouri 63101

1-800-532-6459

http://www.children-cancer.com

The National Cancer Institute

9000 Rockville Pike

Bethesda, Maryland 20892

1-800-422-6237

http://www.cancer.gov

Books

Baker, Lynn S. *You and Leukemia: A Day At a Time*.
  Philadelphia, PA: Saunders, 2002.

Keene, Nancy. *Childhood Leukemia: A Guide for Families,
  Friends, and Caregivers (3rd Edition)*. Sebastopol, CA:
  Patient-Centered Guides, 2002.

Lilleyman, John S. *Childhood Leukemia: The Facts*. New York:
  Oxford University Press, 2000.

Woznick, Leigh A., and Goodheart, Carol D. *Living With
  Childhood Cancer: A Practical Guide to Help Families Cope*.
  Arlington, VA: American Psychological Association, 2001.

Web Sites

Candlelighters Childhood Cancer Foundation
http://www.candlelighters.org

KidsHealth for Kids
http://kidshealth.org/kid/health_problems/cancer/cancer_
  kinds.html

Leukemia Research Foundation
http://www.leukemia-research.org/patient

KidsCourageous
http://www.texaschildrenshospital.org/CareCenters/
  KidsCourageous/Default.aspx

ABOUT THE AUTHOR

Lorrie Klosterman is a biologist and writer who fell in love with cells the first time she viewed them with a microscope. She writes and teaches about health and science for all ages.